THE OFFICIAL
CRYSTAL PALACE
ANNUAL 2024

WRITTEN BY ANDREW MCSTEEN
DESIGNED BY MATTHEW KING

A Grange Publication

© 2023. Published by Grange Communications Ltd., Edinburgh, under licence from Crystal Palace Football Club. Printed in the EU.

Every effort has been made to ensure the accuracy of information within this publication, but the publishers cannot be held responsible for any errors or omissions. Views expressed are those of the author and do not necessarily represent those of the publishers or the football club. All rights reserved.

Photo Credits: Sebastian Frej (Crystal Palace F.C.), Stephen Flynn (Crystal Palace F.C. Women), Neil Everitt, Chris Smith (Brickstand), Pinnacle Photo Agency Ltd (PPAUK), Dan Weir (Crystal Pix), The FA/Getty Images, Getty Images

Thanks: Foz Bowers, James Woodroof, Robin Johnson, Will Robinson, Toby Jagmohan, Gary Issott, Chris Grierson, Ebere Eze, Matt Franks, Terry Byfield, Sammy Brough, Sebastian Frej, Kimberley Vogel, Leigh Nicol, Stephen Flynn, Michael Cuell, Tommy Macarthur, Richard Bamber, Nick Veevers, Chris Smith, Christopher Sleet, Philip Mingo, Dan Weir, Phil Morgan, Rebecca Lowe, Alex Howell, Neil Everitt, Reverend Nigel Sands, Dajon Golding, Karen Amaradivakara.

ISBN: 978-1-915879-16-5

CONTENTS

Club Information and Honours

The 2023/24 Official Crystal Palace Kit

2023/24 Opponents

Palace Men's Squad 2023/24

Palace Women's Squad 2023/24

Classic Shirts

Crystal Palace Men's Season Review 2022/23

Crystal Palace Women's Season Review 2022/23

Quiz: Wordsearch

In Focus: Premier League Goal Celebrations

2022/23: The Best

Make It Happen: Football Reporter

Academy: Building For The Future

Academy: U18s

Academy: U21s

Palace Academy: PL International Cup

Crystal Palace F.C. Women

Palace In The USA

Ted Lasso

Classic Celebrations

World Cup Palace

Eze Skills: Body Feints

Palace For Life Foundation

Behind-The-Scenes: Player Signing On Social

Palace TV Commentary

Quiz: Spot The Ball

Lego Palace

Goodbye and Thanks!

The Art Of The Assist: Michael Olise

Palace History: The Managers

Colour In: Pete & Alice The Eagle

Quiz: Spot The Difference

The Fans

Quiz Answers

Can You Find Pete And Alice The Eagle? Maybe Even A Palace Player Or Two?

CLUB INFORMATION AND HONOURS

Full name: Crystal Palace Football Club
Founded: 1861 (amateur), 1905 (professional)
Nickname: The Eagles
Ground: Selhurst Park
Capacity: 25,486
Opened: August 1924
Address: Whitehorse Lane, London, England, SE25 6PU

ONLINE

Website: www.cpfc.co.uk
Facebook: @officialcpfc
Instagram: @cpfc
Twitter: @cpfc
TikTok: @cpfc
YouTube: @OfficialCPFC

HONOURS

Top-flight (Division One/Premier League)
Best finish: Third - 1990/91

Second tier (Division Two/Championship)
Champions: 1978/79, 1993/94
Runners-up: 1968/69
Play-off winners: 1988/89, 1996/97, 2003/04, 2012/13

FA Cup
Runners-up: 1990, 2016
Semi-finalists: 1976, 1995, 2022

League Cup
Semi-finalists: 1993, 1995, 2001, 2012

Zenith Data Systems Cup
Winners: 1991

FA Youth Cup
Winners: 1977, 1978
Runners-up: 1992, 1997

Premier League International Cup
Runners-up: 2023

INDIVIDUAL RECORDS
APPEARANCES

Most senior appearances
660 - Jim Cannon (1973-1988)

Most consecutive appearances
254 - John Jackson

Youngest first-team player
John Bostock - 15 years, 287 days (v Watford, 29th October 2007)

Oldest first-team player
Jack Little - 41 years, 68 days (v Gillingham, 3rd April 1926)

Longest serving manager
Edmund Goodman - 18 years (1907-1925)

GOALS

Most goals scored (all competitions)
165 - Peter Simpson (1929-35)

Most league goals in a top-flight season
21 - Andrew Johnson (2004/05)

Most goals scored in a league game
6 - Peter Simpson (v Exeter (H) 4th October 1930)

Fastest goal
6 seconds - Keith Smith (v Derby County (A) 12th December 1964)

INTERNATIONAL

Most capped international while at club
55 caps - Wayne Hennessey (Wales)

Highest international goalscorer while at club
11 goals - Christian Benteke (Belgium)

CLUB RECORDS

Biggest Home League Win
9-0 (v Barrow, 10th October 1959)

Biggest Away League Win
6-0 (v Exeter, 26th January 1935; v Birmingham City, 5th September 1987)

Heaviest Home League Defeat
0-7 (v Liverpool, 19th December 2020)

Heaviest Away League Defeat
0-9 (v Liverpool, 11th September 1989)

Most Consecutive Victories
17 (14th October 1905 – 7th April 1906)

RECORD ATTENDANCES AT SELHURST PARK

Top-flight: 49,498 v Chelsea (27th December 1969)
Second tier: 51,482 v Burnley (11th May 1979)

THE 2023/24 OFFICIAL
CRYSTAL PALACE KIT

On the 10-year anniversary since the club were promoted back to the Premier League, the 2023/24 Macron home kit was worn for the first time against Nottingham Forest in May 2023.

The home kit returns to red and blue halves and features a silhouette of the original Crystal Palace building, where the club was founded in 1861 and played from the same year. It is completed by blue shorts with red stripes at the sides and blue socks with two thin lines in red and white around the fold.

The away kit is a union of the club's history and popular sash design from the 1970s. The sash is printed with the words 'Crystal Palace Football Club Founded 1861', in recognition of the club's pivotal role in developing modern football, as the oldest league club in existence still playing professional football.

The main colours – sky blue and white – reference the 1862 club kit colours and are paired with white shorts and white socks topped by a blue band. It was worn for the first time in the pre-season friendly against Barnet in July 2023.

For the goalkeepers, the home kit is eye-catching green and the away kit is purple.

The third kit features south London-inspired graffiti prominently, with dye-sub graphics containing the words 'SOUTH LONDON & PROUD' amalgamated with street-art designs to represent the club's SE25 roots. The shirt is trimmed in red on its right-hand side, and blue on its left, with these colours also appearing on the sleeve cuff and sides.

AFC BOURNEMOUTH
Established: 1899
Nickname: The Cherries
Ground: Vitality Stadium
Capacity: 11,307
Built: 1910
Pitch size: 105m x 68m
Last season: 15th
Premier League Head-to-Head:
Played 12 Won 6 Drawn 4 Lost 2
Website: www.afcb.co.uk
Instagram: @officialafcb

ARSENAL
Established: 1886
Nickname: The Gunners
Ground: Emirates Stadium
Capacity: 60,704
Built: 2006
Pitch size: 105m x 68m
Last season: 2nd
Premier League Head-to-Head:
Played 28 Won 4 Drawn 8 Lost 16
Website: www.arsenal.com
Instagram: @arsenal

ASTON VILLA
Established: 1874
Nickname: The Villans
Ground: Villa Park
Capacity: 42,657
Opened: 1897
Pitch size: 105m x 68m
Last season: 7th
Premier League Head-to-Head:
Played 22 Won 8 Drawn 6 Lost 8
Website: www.avfc.co.uk
Instagram: @avfcofficial

BRENTFORD
Established: 1889
Nickname: The Bees
Ground: Brentford Community Stadium
Capacity: 17,250
Built: 2020
Pitch size: 105m x 68m
Last season: 9th
Premier League Head-to-Head:
Played 4 Won 0 Drawn 4 Lost 0
Website: www.brentfordfc.com
Instagram: @brentfordfc

BRIGHTON AND HOVE ALBION
Established: 1901
Nickname: The Seagulls
Ground: Amex Stadium
Capacity: 31,780
Built: 2011
Pitch size: 105m x 68m
Last season: 6th
Premier League Head-to-Head:
Played 12 Won 3 Drawn 6 Lost 3
Website:
www.brightonandhovealbion.com
Instagram: @officialbhafc

BURNLEY
Established: 1882
Nickname: Clarets
Ground: Turf Moor
Capacity: 21,944
Built: 1883
Pitch size: 105m x 68m
Last season: EFL Championship
Champions (Promoted)
Premier League Head-to-Head:
Played 14 Won 5 Drawn 3 Lost 6
Website: www.burnleyfootballclub.com
Instagram: @burnleyofficial

CHELSEA
Established: 1905
Nickname: The Blues
Ground: Stamford Bridge
Capacity: 40,343
Built: 1877
Pitch size: 103m x 67.5m
Last season: 12th
Premier League Head-to-Head:
Played 28 Won 4 Drawn 2 Lost 22
Website: www.chelseafc.com
Instagram: @chelseafc

EVERTON

Established: 1878
Nickname: The Toffees
Ground: Goodison Park
Capacity: 39,414
Built: 1892
Pitch size: 100.48m x 68m
Last season: 17th
Premier League Head-to-Head:
Played 28 Won 6 Drawn 9 Lost 13
Website: www.evertonfc.com
Instagram: @everton

FULHAM

Established: 1879
Nickname: The Cottagers
Ground: Craven Cottage
Capacity: 22,384
Opened: 1896
Pitch size: 100m x 65m
Last season: 10th
Premier League Head-to-Head:
Played 10 Won 4 Drawn 3 Lost 3
Website: www.fulhamfc.com
Instagram: @fulhamfc

LIVERPOOL

Established: 1892
Nickname: The Reds
Ground: Anfield
Capacity: 53,394
Built: 1884
Pitch size: 101m x 68m
Last season: 5th
Premier League Head-to-Head:
Played 28 Won 5 Drawn 5 Lost 18
Website: www.liverpoolfc.com
Instagram: @liverpoolfc

LUTON TOWN

Established: 1885
Nickname: The Hatters
Ground: Kenilworth Road
Capacity: 10,073
Opened: 1905
Pitch size: 101m x 66m
Last season: EFL Championship: Play-Off Winners (Promoted)
Premier League Head-to-Head:
never played
Website: www.lutontown.co.uk
Instagram: @lutontown

MANCHESTER CITY

Established: 1887
Nickname: The Citizens
Ground: Etihad Stadium
Capacity: 53,400
Built: 2002
Pitch size: 105m x 68m
Last season: 1st/Champions
Premier League Head-to-Head:
Played 26 Won 4 Drawn 6 Lost 16
Website: www.mancity.com
Instagram: @mancity

MANCHESTER UNITED

Established: 1878
Nickname: Red Devils
Ground: Old Trafford
Capacity: 74,310
Built: 1909
Pitch size: 105m x 68m
Last season: 3rd
Premier League Head-to-Head:
Played 28 Won 3 Drawn 6 Lost 19
Website: www.manutd.com
Instagram: @manchesterunited

NEWCASTLE UNITED

Established: 1892
Nickname: The Magpies
Ground: St. James' Park
Capacity: 52,305
Built: 1892 (expanded 2000)
Pitch size: 105m x 68m
Last season: 4th
Premier League Head-to-Head:
Played 24 Won 5 Drawn 8 Lost 11
Website: www.nufc.co.uk
Instagram: @nufc

NOTTINGHAM FOREST

Established: 1865
Nickname: Forest
Ground: The City Ground
Capacity: 30,332
Opened: 1898
Pitch size: 102m x 68m
Last season: 16th
Premier League Head-to-Head:
Played 6 Won 0 Drawn 3 Lost 3
Website: www.nottinghamforest.co.uk
Instagram: @officialnffc

SHEFFIELD UNITED

Established: 1889
Nickname: The Blades
Ground: Bramall Lane
Capacity: 32,050
Opened: 1855
Pitch size: 102m x 66m
Last season: EFL Championship Runners-Up (Promoted)
Premier League Head-to-Head:
Played 6 Won 4 Drawn 0 Lost 2
Website: www.sufc.co.uk
Instagram: @sheffieldunited

TOTTENHAM HOTSPUR

Established: 1882
Nickname: Spurs
Ground: Tottenham Hotspur Stadium
Capacity: 62,850
Built: 2019
Pitch size: 105m x 68m
Last season: 8th
Premier League Head-to-Head:
Played 28 Won 4 Drawn 7 Lost 17
Website: www.tottenhamhotspur.com
Instagram: @spursofficial

WEST HAM UNITED

Established: 1895
Nickname: The Hammers
Ground: London Stadium
Capacity: 60,000
Built: 2011
Pitch size: 105m x 68m
Last season: 14th
Premier League Head-to-Head:
Played 24 Won 8 Drawn 7 Lost 9
Website: www.whufc.com
Instagram: @westham

WOLVERHAMPTON WANDERERS

Established: 1877
Nickname: Wolves
Ground: Molineux Stadium
Capacity: 32,750
Built: 1889
Pitch size: 105m x 68m
Last season: 13th
Premier League Head-to-Head:
Played 10 Won 5 Drawn 1 Lost 4
Website: www.wolves.co.uk
Instagram: @wolves

PALACE MEN'S SQUAD 2023/24

GOALKEEPERS

1

SAM JOHNSTONE
Country: England
Date of Birth: 25/03/1993
Signed: 01/07/2022
Twitter: @samjohnstone
Instagram: @samjohnstone

30

DEAN HENDERSON
Country: England
Date of Birth: 12/03/1997
Signed: 31/08/2023
Twitter: @deanhenderson
Instagram: @deanhenderson

DEFENDERS

31

REMI MATTHEWS
Country: England
Date of Birth: 10/02/1994
Signed: 13/07/2021
Twitter: @remi_matthews
Instagram: @remimatthews

2

JOEL WARD
Country: England
Date of Birth: 29/10/1989
Signed: 29/05/2012
Twitter: @JoelWard2
Instagram: @JoelWard2

3

TYRICK MITCHELL
Country: England
Date of Birth: 01/09/1999
Signed: 01/06/2016
Twitter: @MitchellTyrick
Instagram: @TMitch.27

4

ROB HOLDING
Country: England
Date of Birth: 20/09/1995
Signed: 01/09/2023
Twitter: @robholding95
Instagram: @rholding95

5

JAMES TOMKINS
Country: England
Date of Birth: 29/03/1989
Signed: 05/06/2016

All information correct as of 04/09/23

MARC GUÉHI
Country: England
Date of Birth: 13/07/2000
Signed: 18/07/2021

JOACHIM ANDERSEN
Country: Denmark
Date of Birth: 31/05/1996
Signed: 28/07/2021
Instagram: @JoachimAndersen3

NATHANIEL CLYNE
Country: England
Date of Birth: 05/04/1991
Signed: 14/10/2020
Twitter: @Nathaniel_Clyne
Instagram: @Nathaniel_Clyne

MIDFIELDERS

CHRIS RICHARDS
Country: United States of America
Date of Birth: 28/03/2000
Signed: 27/07/2022
Twitter: @eastmamba
Instagram: @eastmamba

NATHAN FERGUSON
Country: England
Date of Birth: 06/10/2000
Signed: 27/07/2020
Twitter: @Nathan6Ferguson
Instagram: @Nath.Ferguson

MICHAEL OLISE
Country: France
Date of Birth: 12/12/2001
Signed: 08/07/2021
Instagram: @M.Olise

JEFFERSON LERMA
Country: Colombia
Date of Birth: 25/10/1994
Signed: 01/07/2023
Instagram: @jeffersonlerma

EBERECHI EZE
Country: England
Date of Birth: 29/06/1998
Signed: 28/08/2020
Twitter: @EbereEze10
Instagram: @Ebere10

JEFFREY SCHLUPP
Country: Ghana
Date of Birth: 23/12/1992
Signed: 13/01/2017
Twitter: @Jeffrey_Schlupp
Instagram: @JeffreySchlupp

WILL HUGHES
Country: England
Date of Birth: 17/04/1995
Signed: 28/08/2021
Twitter: @wjhughes19

MALCOLM EBIOWEI
Country: England
Date of Birth: 04/09/2003
Signed: 01/07/2022
Twitter: @malcolmebiowei
Instagram: @malcolmebiowei

CHEICK DOUCOURÉ
Country: Mali
Date of Birth: 08/01/2000
Signed: 11/07/2022
Twitter: @C_DoucoureOff
Instagram: @cheick.doucoure20

FORWARDS

NAOUIROU AHAMADA
Country: France
Date of Birth: 29/03/2002
Signed: 31/01/2023
Instagram: @naouirahamada

JAÏRO RIEDEWALD
Country: Netherlands
Date of Birth: 09/09/1996
Signed: 24/07/2017
Instagram: @jriedewald

JORDAN AYEW
Country: Ghana
Date of Birth: 11/09/1991
Signed/From: 25/07/2019
Twitter: @Jordan_Ayew9
Instagram: @JordanAyew9

MATHEUS FRANÇA
Country: Brazil
Date of Birth: 01/04/2004
Signed: 05/08/2023
Instagram: @matheus_franca04

JEAN-PHILIPPE MATETA
Country: France
Date of Birth: 28/06/1997
Signed/From: 21/01/2021 (on loan),
31/01/2022 Permanent
Twitter: @MatetaJPhilippe
Instagram: @IAmMateta

ODSONNE ÉDOUARD
Country: France
Date of Birth: 16/01/1998
Signed: 31/08/2021
Twitter : @oedouard22
Instagram: @o.edouard_18

2

JOEL
WARD

PALACE WOMEN'S

GOALKEEPERS

FRAN KITCHING
Country: England
Date of Birth: 17/02/1998
Signed: 01/07/2022
Twitter: @FranKitching
Instagram: @FranKitching98

NATALIA NEGRI
Country: England
Date of Birth: 02/01/2004
Signed: 01/07/2022
Instagram: @natalianegriii

DEFENDERS

ANNABEL JOHNSON
Country: England
Date of Birth: 20/10/1993
Signed: 01/07/2018
Twitter: @annabelj0hnson
Instagram: @annabelj0hnson

FELICITY GIBBONS
Country: England
Date of Birth: 09/07/1994
Signed: 01/07/2022

AIMEE EVERETT
Country: England
Date of Birth: 02/08/2001
Signed: 01/07/2021
Twitter: @aimee_everett
Instagram: @aimee.everett

KIRSTEN REILLY
Country: Scotland
Date of Birth: 20/08/1995
Signed: 01/07/2022
Twitter: @kirstenreilly16
Instagram: @kirstenreilly

LIA CATALDO
Country: England
Date of Birth: 11/02/2001
Signed: 01/07/2023
Twitter: @LiaCataldo
Instagram: @LiaMartinaCataldo

HAYLEY NOLAN
Country: Ireland
Date of Birth: 07/03/1997
Signed: 01/07/2023
Twitter: @Hayley__Nolan
Instagram: @Hayley__Nolan

POLLY DORAN
Country: Australia
Date of Birth: 05/09/2001
Signed: 01/07/2022
Twitter: @polly_doran
Instagram: @polly.doran

SQUAD 2023/24

MIDFIELDERS

(4)

CHLOE ARTHUR
Country: Scotland
Date of Birth: 21/01/1995
Signed: 01/07/2022
Instagram: @chloearthur77

(5)

ANNA FILBEY
Country: Wales
Date of Birth: 11/10/1999
Signed: 01/07/2022
Twitter: @anna_filbey99
Instagram: @annafilbey

(16)

ELLIE NOBLE
Country: England
Date of Birth: 12/09/1999
Signed: 01/07/2022
Twitter: @ellienoble4

FORWARDS

(21)

SHAUNA GUYATT
Country: England
Date of Birth: 14/02/2005
Signed: 01/07/2022
Instagram: @shauna.guyatt

(24)

SHANADE HOPCROFT
Country: England
Date of Birth: 04/10/1997
Signed: 01/07/2023
Twitter: @shanadehopcroft
Instagram: @shanadehopcroft

(8)

MOLLY-MAE SHARPE
Country: England
Date of Birth: 12/03/1998
Signed: 01/07/2021
Twitter: @mollysharpe_
Instagram: @mollysharpe_

(9)

ELISE HUGHES
Country: Wales
Date of Birth: 15/04/2001
Signed: 01/07/2022
Twitter: @elise__hughes
Instagram: @elise__hughes

(10)

ANNABEL BLANCHARD
Country: England
Date of Birth: 07/05/2001
Signed: 01/07/2022
Twitter: @annabelblanch10
Instagram: @annabelblanchard

(14)

PAIGE BAILEY-GAYLE
Country: Jamaica
Date of Birth: 12/11/2001
Signed: 01/07/2022
Twitter: @paigebgayle
Instagram: @paigebgayle

CLASSIC SHIRTS

PREMIER LEAGUE

Played 38 **Won** 11 **Drawn** 12 **Lost** 15 **Goals For** 40 **Goals Against** 49 **Clean Sheets** 9
Goals per match 1.05 **Total passes** 15,707 **Position:** 11th **Top Goalscorer:** Ebere Eze (10)
Most Appearances: Jordan Ayew, Ebere Eze (38) **Managers:** Patrick Vieira, Paddy McCarthy, Roy Hodgson

Friday 5 August
CRYSTAL PALACE 0-2 ARSENAL
Martinelli 20,
Guéhi 85 (og)

After nine friendlies split between two squads playing in three continents, the Eagles and boss Patrick Vieira finally got together and started their 2022/23 Premier League campaign. It was an earlier-than-usual start to the season due to the upcoming winter break for the 2022 FIFA World Cup, with Palace going down 2-0. Cheick Doucouré made his Premier League debut for Palace.

Saturday 20 August
CRYSTAL PALACE 3-1 ASTON VILLA
Zaha 7, 58,   Watkins 5
Mateta 71

Despite going behind early on, the home side immediately replied, through Zaha, who doubled his account in the second-half after slotting home following a penalty save. A Jean-Philippe Mateta strike secured victory.

Monday 15 August
LIVERPOOL 1-1 CRYSTAL PALACE
Diaz 61   Zaha 32

A sublime Ebere Eze assist saw Wilfried Zaha put the visitors ahead at Anfield, but the home side equalised. USA defender Chris Richards made his debut for Vieira's side.

Saturday 27 August
MANCHESTER CITY 4-2 CRYSTAL PALACE
Bernardo Silva 53,   Stones 4 (og),
Haaland 62, 70, 81   Andersen 21

Eventual champions Manchester City were shocked early on at home with the Eagles going 2-0 up just past the 20-minute mark, but an Erling Haaland second-half hat-trick ensured a home win.

Tuesday 30 August
CRYSTAL PALACE 1-1 BRENTFORD
Zaha 59   Wissa 88

A late Brentford equaliser cancelled out a stunning strike from Zaha as the points were shared.

Saturday 3 September
NEWCASTLE UNITED 0-0 CRYSTAL PALACE

With a sterling display in the Palace goal, Vicente Guaita ensured a point for the Eagles was gathered in the north-east.

Saturday 1 October
CRYSTAL PALACE 1-2 CHELSEA
Édouard 7   Aubameyang 38,
                        Gallagher 90

Former Palace loanee Conor Gallagher returned and scored a last-minute winners after Édouard gave the SE25 side an early lead. Chelsea defender Thiago Silva avoided a red card after preventing Jordan Ayew racing through on goal.

Sunday 9 October
CRYSTAL PALACE 2-1 LEEDS UNITED
Édouard 24,   Struijk 10
Eze 76

Vieira's side fought back to take all three points thanks to an Eze winner after Édouard had brought the teams level.

Saturday 15 October
LEICESTER CITY 0-0 CRYSTAL PALACE

The Eagles could not find the net against the bottom side with Guaita in the Palace goal making a number of crucial saves again.

Tuesday 18 October
CRYSTAL PALACE 2-1 WOLVERHAMPTON WANDERERS
Eze 47,   Traoré 31
Zaha 70

A powerful header from Adama Traoré put the visitors up and they hit the post late on in the first-half, but the home team came out strong in the second-half, Eze equalising early on and then a low, winning strike from Zaha which put his side into the top 10.

Saturday 22 October

EVERTON 3-0 CRYSTAL PALACE

Calvert-Lewin 11,
Gordon 63,
McNeil 84

A disappointing performance in Merseyside saw the Eagles suffer their joint-second biggest defeat of the season.

Sunday 6 November

WEST HAM UNITED 1-2 CRYSTAL PALACE

Benrahma 20
Zaha 41,
Olise 90+4

A 90+4 strike from Michael Olise – which would go on to win 'Moment of the Season' at the end of season awards – saw the Eagles come from behind again to win. Eze had supplied Zaha to score the earlier equaliser.

Saturday 29 October

CRYSTAL PALACE 1-0 SOUTHAMPTON

Édouard 38

The Eagles made it three wins in a row at home after an Odsonne Édouard first-half strike which had followed a disallowed goal moments earlier for offside.

Saturday 12 November

NOTTINGHAM FOREST 1-0 CRYSTAL PALACE

Gibbs-White 54

In the last match before a six-week break due to the 2022 FIFA World Cup in Qatar, a Zaha missed first-half penalty was punished by a Morgan Gibbs-White early second-half goal to hand the home side all three points.

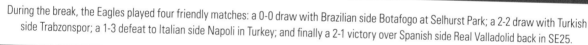

During the break, the Eagles played four friendly matches: a 0-0 draw with Brazilian side Botafogo at Selhurst Park; a 2-2 draw with Turkish side Trabzonspor; a 1-3 defeat to Italian side Napoli in Turkey; and finally a 2-1 victory over Spanish side Real Valladolid back in SE25.

Monday 26 December

CRYSTAL PALACE 0-3 FULHAM

De Cordova-Reid 31,
Ream 71,
Mitrović 80

Palace returned to Premier League action after almost seven weeks and handed the visitors some Christmas presents as they went down to nine men after Tyrick Mitchell and James Tomkins were sent off. Jordan Ayew had hit the crossbar early on.

Saturday 31 December

BOURNEMOUTH 0-2 CRYSTAL PALACE

Ayew 19,
Eze 36

A dominant 2-0 away win on the south coast thanks to first-half goals from Ayew and Eze would be the last win for the Eagles until 1 April 2023 and the last under Vieira.

Wednesday 4 January
CRYSTAL PALACE 0-4 TOTTENHAM HOTSPUR

Kane 48, 53,
Doherty 68,
Son 72

Palace were handed their biggest defeat of the season after Spurs scored four second-half goals. Ahead of the game tributes were paid to Eagles goalkeeper John Jackson and musician and Palace supporter, director and musician Maxi Jazz, who had sadly both passed away over the festive period.

Sunday 15 January
CHELSEA 1-0 CRYSTAL PALACE
Havertz 64

Chelsea completed the league double over their SE25 rivals thanks to a second-half Kai Havertz goal.

Wednesday 18 January
CRYSTAL PALACE 1-1 MANCHESTER UNITED
Olise 90+1   Fernandes 44

A 30-yard, stoppage time free-kick from Michael Olise shocked Erik Ten Hag and his Manchester United squad as Palace put an end to their losing ways under the floodlights. The goal would later win 'Goal of the Season' at the end of season awards. Chris Richards made his first Premier League start in place of an injured Joachim Andersen.

Saturday 21 January
CRYSTAL PALACE 0-0 NEWCASTLE UNITED

A third goalless draw of the season against the Champions League-chasing side saw Zaha make his 450th appearance for the Eagles. Academy prospect David Ozoh came on as a 90th-minute sub to become Palace's youngest-ever Premier League player at the age of 17 years, eight months and 15 days old.

Saturday 4 February
MANCHESTER UNITED 2-1 CRYSTAL PALACE
Fernandes 7 (p),   Schlupp 76
Rashford 62

Jeff Schlupp's goal 15 minutes from the end was not enough to grab a crucial away point at Old Trafford. January transfer window signing Naouirou Ahamada and loan signing from Arsenal, Sambi Lokonga, made their debuts for the Eagles.

Saturday 11 February
CRYSTAL PALACE 1-1 BRIGHTON & HOVE ALBION
Tomkins 69   March 63

In just his fourth league appearance of the season, James Tomkins scored his first goal since December 2021 to cancel out Solly March's opener.

Saturday 18 February

BRENTFORD 1-1 CRYSTAL PALACE
Janelt 90+6   Eze 69

With virtually the last kick of the game, Brentford cancelled out Eze's 69th minute opener. Palace played in their black third kit for the first time.

Saturday 25 February

CRYSTAL PALACE 0-0 LIVERPOOL

A second draw of the season against Liverpool saw the home side fail to convert numerous chances and survive a late miss from the visitors' Cody Gakpo thanks to some good goalkeeping from Guaita.

Saturday 4 March

ASTON VILLA 1-0 CRYSTAL PALACE
Andersen 27 (og)

Joachim Andersen's own goal saw Palace slip to defeat at Villa Park. Zaha was denied a superb goal on his return to action, following injury, by VAR. Doucouré was dismissed after an hour, following two yellow cards in quick succession.

Saturday 11 March

CRYSTAL PALACE 0-1 MANCHESTER CITY
Haaland 78 (p)

Erling Haaland's penalty saw Crystal Palace lose out to City, their 11th game in a row without a win. It would prove to be Vieira's last home game.

Wednesday 15 March

BRIGHTON & HOVE ALBION 1-0 CRYSTAL PALACE
March 15

In what would be Vieira's last game in charge Brighton took a 1-0 win with Palace Academy graduate and lifelong fan Joe Whitworth becoming Palace's youngest Premier League goalkeeper at 19 years and 15 days old.

Sunday 19 March

ARSENAL 4-1 CRYSTAL PALACE
Martinelli 28,   Schlupp 63
Saka 43, 74,
Xhaka 55

Paddy McCarthy took the reins as caretaker manager with Whitworth continuing in goal, but the North Londoners were already 3-0 up before Schlupp gave the visitors a glimmer of hope.

Saturday 1 April
CRYSTAL PALACE 2-1 LEICESTER CITY
Iversen 59 (og),   Pereira 56
Mateta 90+4

With Premier League safety not secure, 10 games remaining and a short break in action, Palace Chairman Steve Parish brought back previous manager Roy Hodgson for the rest of the season. His second spell in charge got off to the best possible start as Jean-Philippe Mateta grabbed a precious three points in injury time, following an earlier, deflected Eze free-kick strike.

Sunday 9 April
LEEDS UNITED 1-5 CRYSTAL PALACE
Bamford 21   Guéhi 45+1,
                    Ayew 53, 77,
                    Eze 55,
                    Édouard 69

The Eagles recorded their biggest win of the season with a five-star performance featuring three assists by Michael Olise. Sam Johnstone made his first league start of the season.

Saturday 15 April
SOUTHAMPTON 0-2 CRYSTAL PALACE
                    Eze 54, 68

Eze scored two classy goals against the relegation-threatened Saints to make it three wins in a row for the Eagles under Hodgson.

Saturday 22 April
CRYSTAL PALACE 0-0 EVERTON

An unchanged Eagles side peppered the Evertonian goal but the Sean Dyche-led, relegation-threatened Toffees held firm.

Tuesday 25 April
WOLVERHAMPTON WANDERERS 2-0 CRYSTAL PALACE
Andersen 3 (og),
Neves 90+4 (p)

Hodgson rested key players in a busy period but it was a night to forget for the travelling fans as an early Andersen own goal and late penalty ensured a frustrating evening for the Eagles.

Saturday 29 April
CRYSTAL PALACE 4-3 WEST HAM UNITED
Ayew 15,   Soucek 9,
Zaha 20,   Antonio 35,
Schlupp 30,   Aguerd 72
Eze 66

The Eagles bounced back as Zaha scored on his return from a four-week injury to help Palace secure victory. The two teams traded goals in south London but Palace came out on top to move up to 11th place in the table.

Saturday 6 May
TOTTENHAM HOTSPUR 1-0 CRYSTAL PALACE
Kane 45+1

Harry Kane's powerful header in first-half stoppage time consigned Palace to defeat, but results elsewhere ensured Premier League safety for another season.

Saturday 20 May
FULHAM 2-2 CRYSTAL PALACE
Mitrović   Édouard 34,
45+5 (p), 61   Ward 83

Joel Ward scored his first Crystal Palace goal since 2019 as his side came from behind again to earn a point at Craven Cottage.

Saturday 13 May
CRYSTAL PALACE 2-0 BOURNEMOUTH
Eze 39, 58

The Eagles completed the league double over Bournemouth as Eze's end-of-season form went up another notch. His second was a wonder-goal to reflect the Eagles' dominance. The result moved Palace above Chelsea in the table, into 11th, a position they would finish the season in.

Sunday 28 May
CRYSTAL PALACE 1-1 NOTTINGHAM FOREST
Hughes 66   Awoniyi 31

The longest Premier League season in its 30-year history came to an end with a draw thanks to a Will Hughes second-half header, his first league goal for the Eagles. Two former Palace captains appeared at Selhurst Park for the last time with James McArthur and Luka Milivojević receiving special presentations on the pitch.

LEAGUE CUP & FA CUP

League Cup 2nd Round
Tuesday 23 August
OXFORD UNITED 0-2 CRYSTAL PALACE
Édouard 71,
Milivojević 90 (p)

Vieira made nine changes to his squad, handing debuts to new signing Sam Johnstone, plus youth prospects Kaden Rodney and Killian Phillips.

League Cup 3rd Round
Wednesday 9 November
NEWCASTLE UNITED 0-0 CRYSTAL PALACE
Newcastle win 3-2 on penalties

Luka Milivojević, Jean-Philippe Mateta and finally Malcolm Ebiowei all missed penalties as Palace went out.

FA Cup Third Round
Saturday 7 January
CRYSTAL PALACE 1-2 SOUTHAMPTON
Édouard 14   Ward-Prowse 37,
              Armstrong 68

The Eagles were knocked out of the FA Cup at the first time of asking, despite taking an early lead.

WOMEN'S SEASON REVIEW 2022/23

Off the back of a record-breaking 2021/22 campaign which saw them finish fourth in the Women's Championship, Crystal Palace Women kicked-off the 2022/23 season with 15 new signings in their matchday squad.

And it got off to a brilliant start, as Issy Sibley's second-half strike sealed all three points against London City Lionesses at Princes Park Stadium. The game saw eight players make their Palace debuts.

Despite early cup exits, the league season would end with a fifth-place finish in the ultra-competitive league.

The season featured memorable moments, including a then-record attendance of 1,876 at Selhurst Park in September. Palace returned to Selhurst for a south London derby against Charlton Athletic in November which broke the attendance record again, this time with 1,969 supporters in attendance.

Women's Football Weekend in March was cause to celebrate in Bromley with a bumper crowd of over 1,700 in attendance at Hayes Lane treated to a 1-0 win over Blackburn Rovers Ladies. It was the club's third highest attendance in history, and highest-ever at their home ground.

The home campaign would end on a high in April as Palace put on a display full of energy and determination to win 4-1 against Lewes in their final match at Hayes Lane and they ended the season with their first draw – a 1-1 away at The Valley, Charlton, and that top-five finish.

A number of players also got international call-ups throughout the season with Elise Hughes and Anna Filbey (Wales), Chloe Arthur (Scotland), Paige Bailey-Gayle (Jamaica) and Natalia Negri, Shauna Guyatt and Isabella Sibley (England) all representing their countries.

RESULTS

Women's Championship
London City Lionesses 0-1 Crystal Palace
Crystal Palace 3-0 Coventry United
Crystal Palace 1-2 Southampton
Blackburn Rovers 1-3 Crystal Palace
Crystal Palace 0-2 Sunderland
Bristol City 3-0 Crystal Palace
Durham 0-1 Crystal Palace
Crystal Palace 1-2 Charlton Athletic
Lewes 0-1 Crystal Palace
Crystal Palace 0-5 London City Lionesses
Coventry United 3-2 Crystal Palace
Southampton 2-0 Crystal Palace
Crystal Palace 1-0 Durham
Crystal Palace 2-1 Sheffield United
Crystal Palace 0-3 Bristol City
Sheffield United 0-1 Crystal Palace
Birmingham City 3-1 Crystal Palace
Crystal Palace 1-0 Blackburn Rovers
Sunderland 1-2 Crystal Palace
Crystal Palace 2-4 Birmingham City
Crystal Palace 4-1 Lewes
Charlton Athletic 1-1 Crystal Palace

Women's League Cup
Bristol City 4-0 Crystal Palace
Crystal Palace 1-4 Lewes
Charlton Athletic 2-0 Crystal Palace

Women's FA Cup
Crystal Palace 5-1 Watford
Durham 3-0 Crystal Palace

WORDSEARCH

CAN YOU FIND THESE 20 CRYSTAL PALACE PLAYERS?

```
K T A Y E W G R L T K R K M Q H
Z R T R F V U K N G V M R N T E
B R W N H H N E N J Z G Q N P N
Z L H L T C G M E X O K K R D D
J R A R P R L P S H T H R P W E
S R A N I K R K R H T E N B C R
N P V M C A M V E X T F Z S K S
O P K Y H H N V D R D V R E O O
B U I S W N A P N R B E M C N N
B L T H Y V B R A H I T I V H L
I H C C T B Y W D L W L T K J H
G C H Q M N R E L L M W C X K Z
E S I L O C K Y B H U G H E S W
G X N N C L B J L T T E P B H
N K G T O M K I N S I Z L D K R
T T E R E V E L T M C F L R R M
```

ANDERSEN	EZE	JOHNSON	REILLY
ARTHUR	FILBEY	KITCHING	SCHLUPP
AYEW	GIBBONS	MITCHELL	SHARPE
BLANCHARD	HENDERSON	NEGRI	TOMKINS
EVERETT	HUGHES	OLISE	WARD

Answers on Page 61!

IN FOCUS: PREMIER LEAGUE GOAL CELEBRATIONS

Last season, the Eagles registered 40 goals in the Premier League which included one own goal from Manchester City's John Stones.

Club photographer Sebastian Frej along with James Fearn and Micah Crook captured them all. Frej talks us through how he captures these special moments.

"I don't speak to players about where they will celebrate, I want them to be spontaneous. I only want them to think about tactics."

"At home games, I move around Selhurst, but at away games, I always sit close to the Palace fans."

"If a goal celebration happens right in front of you, you need a 24-70mm f2.8 lens. If mid-range, a few metres away, then you need a 70-200 mm f2.8 lens. But if you don't have luck and the goal happens far away from you, you need a 500mm f4 lens."

"I have to send goal pictures as soon as possible. If my camera is connected to an internet cable by my laptop where I am sitting, it is not a problem, but if am walking around the stadium or without a cable or strong wi-fi, I will send at half-time or just after full-time."

"When a goal is scored, I need to make quick decision about which lens I will use. Do I want to show the close details of a facial expression? If so, then I stay on a 400 or 500mm lens but I risk missing something."

2022/23 THE BEST

The 2022/23 Crystal Palace F.C. Awards took place in front of hundreds of fans at the Clapham Grand in south London.

MEN'S PLAYER OF THE SEASON
CHEICK DOUCOURÉ

WOMEN'S PLAYER OF THE SEASON
FRAN KITCHING

MEN'S PLAYERS'
PLAYER OF THE SEASON
MICHAEL OLISE

MEN'S GOAL OF THE SEASON
MICHAEL OLISE
v Manchester United (H) – 18 January 2023

MOMENT OF THE SEASON
MICHAEL OLISE'S 94TH-MINUTE
WINNER AGAINST WEST HAM

CHAIRMAN'S AWARD FOR
OUTSTANDING CONTRIBUTION
JAMES MCARTHUR & LUKA MILIVOJEVIĆ

UNDER-18 MEN'S PLAYER OF THE SEASON
ZACH MARSH

PFA COMMUNITY CHAMPIONS
CHLOE ARTHUR & TYRICK MITCHELL

UNDER-21 MEN'S PLAYER OF THE SEASON
DAVID OZOH

MAKE IT HAPPEN: FOOTBALL REPORTER

Ever dreamt of speaking to your favourite football players as your job? Well, Alex Howell does in his role as a Football Reporter for the BBC. Alex grew up in a Crystal Palace supporting family with his dad taking him to his first game, away at Millwall in 1996, as a four-year-old. He shares memories and tips from his career so far…

The BBC

I moved to Manchester to work for the BBC social media team where I covered sporting events for their social accounts. I like to tell stories so I pitched ideas to BBC Football Focus. One was about a player who did WWE celebrations when they scored, they liked it and gave me the opportunity to tell it. I then knew that's what I wanted to do.

Relationships are key

Good relationships mean contacts are more likely to give you information. Without them, you can't really tell stories. When I speak to people, I approach it like a friendship – you keep the conversation going.

Starting out

The first thing I did in media was audition to be the Palace TV presenter in the car park of Selhurst Park. I didn't get the job, but it sparked my interest in the media industry.

Highlights

Working at a FIFA World Cup as the BBC in-camp England reporter is something I dreamt of achieving and I did it for Qatar 2022. I was updating live from England training and games and interviewing players. Harry Kane was a highlight; he speaks very well.

The path

I studied for a journalist qualification before working at a non-football YouTube sports channel. I joined so I could learn the skills needed for my next move, which was joining Crystal Palace where I was in charge of their social media accounts.

Tips

Nobody knows everything, try new things, ask questions and get advice from more experienced people – it's the only way to learn. When I'm telling a story, I think; 'what would I ask if I had no knowledge of this at all?'.

PALACE ACADEMY
BUILDING FOR THE FUTURE

Over 200 young players across 10 teams form the Crystal Palace F.C. Academy in Beckenham, which employs around 50 full-time and 100 part-time staff producing superstar players like Wilfried Zaha, Jesurun Rak-Sakyi and Aaron Wan-Bissaka.

Teams play their home games mainly at Beckenham, but sometimes even at Selhurst Park!

Many former Palace players including Rob Quinn, Julián Speroni and Darren Powell are involved in coaching and managing, all overseen by Academy Director Gary Issott.

The 2022/23 season saw the U12 side win the Mina Cup in Dubai, the U14s reach the MIC Cup quarter-final, the U15s win the national Floodlit Cup and the U16 team end with a 71% win percentage including reaching the semi-finals of the MIC Cup where they lost to FC Barcelona.

You can read about how the U18s and U21s got on over the next three pages…

After being upgraded to Category 1 status in July 2020, the new, upgraded Academy development in Beckenham was officially opened in 2021 by Palace Academy graduate Gareth Southgate.

The site features numerous indoor and outdoor pitches, rehab and gym facilities, offices, restaurant, meeting rooms and much more. It is also the training home for Crystal Palace F.C. Women and regularly hosts a wide range of community events.

A comprehensive Care Programme for Academy players aged 18-23 released from the club is in place with dedicated Player Care Officers in contact with them for an extended period of time.

Together, the Academy and First Team Training Ground are spread over 50 acres right in the heart of south London, providing all the necessary tools for the club to progress to the next level.

THE ACADEMY – UNDER-18s

The 2022/23 season saw the Under-18s record their third successive top-three finish in the U18 Premier League South.

After an opening day loss, Rob Quinn's side won six games in a row and went on to register just one defeat in their last 11 to ensure third place, just a point behind runners-up Fulham, two ahead of Chelsea. A highlight of their season was a 7-1 victory against reigning league champions Southampton.

Their PL Cup exploits ended in November when a four-goal swing in the final round of games saw them knocked out of contention for the next round after earlier topping their group. Reigning champions Manchester United knocked the Eagles out of the FA Youth Cup at Selhurst Park at the first hurdle.

David Ozoh and Kaden Rodney impressed as second-year scholars moving up an age group to play for the Palace U21s. Ozoh would go on to win the U21s' Player of the Season Award and make his Premier League debut, with Rodney also appearing for the first-team in the League Cup.

2022/23 RESULTS

Played: 26, Won: 13, Drew: 6, Lost: 7
Most appearances: Mofe Jemide (25)
Top-scorer: Junior Dixon (12)
Player of the Year: Zach Marsh

INTERNATIONAL HONOURS 2022/23

Franco Umeh: Ireland U19s
Dylan Reid: Scotland U18s (captain)
Zach Marsh: England U18s (scored twice on his first start vs Australia)
Mofe Jemide: England U17s (made the U17 European Championship quarter-finals)
Jake Grante: Ireland U17s (made the U17 European Championship quarter-finals)

THE ACADEMY - UNDER-21s

After two seasons playing as the U23s, the U21s returned for the 2022/23 season.

Competing in four competitions, the Eagles were initially led by Paddy McCarthy as manager before he moved to the first team and was replaced by his assistant Darren Powell.

Their Premier League 2 Division 1 campaign saw them lose just once in their first 11 games, with two losses in their next 12. After losing their final three league games, they finished just one point behind Fulham in third and four behind Liverpool in second, but their fourth-place finish was an improvement on fifth place last season.

In the EFL Trophy they faced the senior teams of Bristol Rovers, Swindon and eventual finalists Plymouth Argyle, before going out at the group stage, while in the Premier League Cup they missed out on qualification from the group stage after facing Sheffield United, Newcastle United and Bristol City home and away.

Read all about the U21 Premier League International Cup run on the next page.

U21 players Joe Whitworth and Killian Phillips joined U18 graduates David Ozoh and Kaden Rodney in making their first team debuts in the 2022/23 season.

2022/23 RESULTS
Played: 42, Won: 19, Drew: 11, Lost: 12
Most appearances: Kaden Rodney (37)
Top-scorer: John Kymani-Gordon (13)
Player of the Year: David Ozoh

INTERNATIONAL HONOURS 2022/23
Tayo Adaramola: Ireland U21s
Seán Grehan: Ireland U19s & U21s
Killian Phillips: Ireland U21s
Jadan Raymond: Wales U21s
David Ozoh: England U18s

Premier League International Cup

The Premier League International Cup is a European club competition featuring players aged 16-21 years old and the Eagles finished as runners-up!

All teams are allowed up to five over-age outfield players and one goalkeeper in their squad with Jaïro Riedewald, Sam Johnstone, Chris Richards and Malcolm Ebiowei featuring across the first three games for Palace.

In the preliminary group stage the Eagles saw off German team Hertha Berlin and French side Paris Saint-Germain, lost to Croatian team Dinamo Zagreb, but defeated Portuguese outfit Braga to qualify for the quarter-finals.

The last eight saw Darren Powell take over as manager from Paddy McCarthy, who was promoted to the first team, and they delivered a 1-0 away win at Liverpool thanks to a first-half goal from Victor Akinwale.

Selhurst Park was the venue for the semi-final clash with Spanish side Valencia and Powell's men won again, taking a 5-3 penalty shoot-out victory after a 1-1 extra-time draw.

This set up a final against Dutch side PSV Eindhoven, 'Jong PSV', but the home side went down 3-1 after extra time in front of 5,941 supporters in SE25.

RESULTS

Preliminary Group C - *Champion Hill, Dulwich*

Tuesday 6 September 2022
CRYSTAL PALACE 1-0 HERTHA BSC
Ola-Adebomi 56

Wednesday 28 September 2022
CRYSTAL PALACE 7-3 PARIS SAINT-GERMAIN
Gordon 16, 23, 61,   Tchicamboud 3, 81,
Akinwale 21,   Mukelenge 66
Omilabu 35,
Cadogan 59,
Mooney 90+1

Saturday 4 February 2023
CRYSTAL PALACE 1-2 DINAMO ZAGREB
Mooney 43,   Brkljaca 14,
                        Ilecic 65

Wednesday 8 February 2023
CRYSTAL PALACE 2-1 BRAGA
Grehan 25,   Lacximicant 9
Wells-Morrison 90+3

Quarter-Final - *Liverpool FC Academy, Kirkby*

Friday 31 March 2023
LIVERPOOL 0-1 CRYSTAL PALACE
                    Akinwale 34

Semi-Final - *Selhurst Park, London*

Wednesday 3 May 2023
CRYSTAL PALACE 1-1 VALENCIA
(AET – Crystal Palace win 5-3 on penalties)
Raymond 18   Gozálbez 68

Final - *Selhurst Park, London*

Tuesday 23 May 2023
CRYSTAL PALACE 1-3 (AET) PSV EINDHOVEN
Banks 42   Sealy 34,
                        van Duiven 99,
                        Colyn 120+1

CRYSTAL PALACE F.C. WOMEN

Crystal Palace F.C. Women were founded in 1992 and are a core part of Crystal Palace Football Club.

The first team play in the FA Women's Championship, one level below the Women's Super League, and for the 2023/24 season will play their home matches at Sutton United's VBS Community Stadium after moving from Hayes Lane, home of Bromley FC, where they had played since 2014.

They train full-time at the Crystal Palace F.C. Academy in Beckenham.

Matchdays are always family-friendly and fun, with children encouraged to attend. Players routinely make time to meet and talk with supporters, as fans get close to the match action.

In addition to the squad (Page 14-15), for the 2023-24 season Chelsea midfielder Lexi Potter and Manchester United striker Keira Barry have joined on season-long loans, while Arsenal winger Araya Dennis has signed dual-registration terms.

CLUB RECORDS
since promotion to Championship 2018/19
Club Founded: 1992

Most appearances (all competitions)
Annabel Johnson: 82
Lizzie Waldie: 74
Coral Haines: 69
Bianca Baptiste: 59

Most goals (all competitions)
Bianca Baptiste: 18
Coral Haines: 17
Molly Sharpe: 12
Siobhan Wilson: 8

Most goals in one season
Bianca Baptiste: 14 (2020/21 - 8 league, 6 cup)

Most clean sheets (in one season)
Fran Kitching: 7

Biggest league win
5-0 vs London Bees (14th February 2021)

Furthest cup round reached
FA Cup: Fifth Round
FA Women's League Cup: Quarter-Final

Biggest attendance at Selhurst Park
Charlton Athletic: 1,969 (18th September 2022)

Current internationals
Shauna Guyatt: England U19
Natalia Negri: England U19
Hayley Nolan: Ireland
Paige Bailey-Gayle: Jamaica
Chloe Arthur: Scotland
Kirsten Reilly: Scotland
Anna Filbey: Wales
Elise Hughes: Wales

LIA CATALDO

- Started in midfield before moving to full-back with right-back preferred position
- Double FA Women's Championship title-winner, with Leicester City and Bristol City
- Has represented England from U16 to U19 level

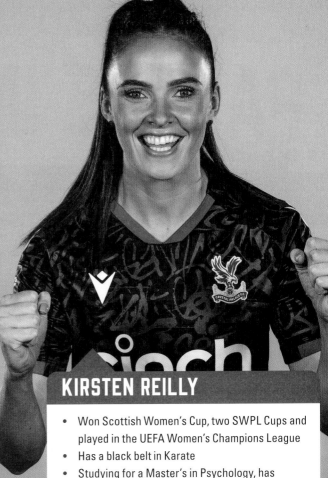

KIRSTEN REILLY

- Won Scottish Women's Cup, two SWPL Cups and played in the UEFA Women's Champions League
- Has a black belt in Karate
- Studying for a Master's in Psychology, has degree in Mathematics

ANNABEL JOHNSON

- Longest-serving player for club
- Played at the 2017 World University Games (Summer Universiade)
- Has degree in Sports Management and Master's in Sports Business Management

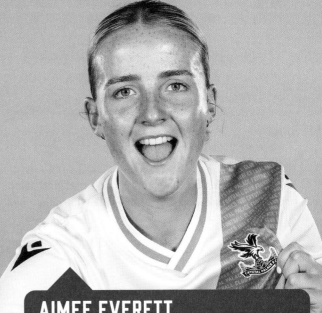

AIMEE EVERETT

- Joined Palace in July 2021 and was named Palace Women's Player of the Season in her first season
- Won both the Women's Championship and Continental Tyres League Cup with Leicester City
- Announced as captain of Crystal Palace Women in August 2023

PALACE IN THE USA

Last summer, both the men's U21s and First Team travelled to the USA to play friendly games.

The First Team returned to the USA for the first time since 2016, facing Millonarios FC in Chicago and Sevilla in Detroit.

The players held open training sessions, questions and answer events, tailgate/fan parties, tasted the famous Chicago deep dish pizza and Coney Island Hot Dogs, met the Detroit Lions NFL team, shot hoops at the Chicago Bulls NBA training facility and even met a real-life American Eagle!

We spoke to some Palace USA fans who were there about why they support the Eagles…

JACQUELINE HARDT, SAN DIEGO

- Born in UK, saw first game in 1980s
- A fourth-generation Palace fan, from a family who have supported the club over 100 years
- Moved to San Diego in 2002, member of San Diego Palace fan club
- Favourite player: Dougie Freedman

What does Crystal Palace mean to you?
"I love the deep connection with my club and the feeling reminds me of my roots."

RICHARD VANREW, COLORADO

- Grew up in Surrey, became fan around the 1990 FA Cup Final
- Used to have season ticket in Lower Holmesdale Block E
- Member of Colorado Palace fan club, runs CPFC USA website
- Favourite players: Andrew Johnson (goals), Ray Houghton (inspirational)

What does Crystal Palace mean to you?
"We're like a big family."

GARRET KOMATZ, DETROIT

› Started being interested in Palace in 2013, full-time Eagle by end of 2015/2016 season
› Been to Selhurst Park twice in 2017 and 2019, both wins
› Administrator for Detroit Eagles fan group
› Favourite player: Ebere Eze

What does Crystal Palace mean to you?
"The experiences I have watching Palace sometimes mirror the experiences I have in life."

JACOB NEWCOMB, BOSTON

› Fell in love with Palace when Premier League games started on American television in 2013
› Watched Palace in Philadelphia in 2016
› Known as "Crystal Palace Fan" on local sports talk radio station
› Favourite players: Julian Speroni, Jonny Williams, Ebere Eze

What does Crystal Palace mean to you?
"They have become part of my identity. Between them, the Boston Red Sox, and Boston Celtics, I feel a sense of family with my team and my fellow fans."

JARED HIMES, COLUMBUS

› Became fan on January 2017 deadline day when Patrick van Aanholt signed
› Been to Selhurst Park and son was a mascot at a game once
› Stands up while watching Palace on TV in America
› Favourite player: Patrick van Aanholt

What does Crystal Palace mean to you?
"Palace means community, heart, resilience, stress and joy."

 Crystal Palace have supporters clubs all around the world, for more information, visit:
www.cpfc.co.uk/supporters/supporting-overseas

THE CHICAGO

TED LASSO

'Ted Lasso' is an American sports TV comedy-drama series, which follows American college football coach 'Ted' who is hired to coach a fictional English football team – AFC Richmond. Played by American actor Jason Sudeikis, Lasso was created back in 2013 to promote the USA TV channel's NBC Sports coverage of the Premier League with a short film released on YouTube.

In 2014 NBC Sports revisited Lasso and this time, lifelong Crystal Palace fan and NBC Premier League host Rebecca Lowe was involved. "The 2013 film went viral so Lasso returned, but this time they wanted me to be in it," said Lowe. "I was trying to act super cool for filming, but there's no script and Jason just said to me, 'we're just going to improvise'. I don't know how I got through it as we had to do so many takes because I couldn't control my laughter. It was incredible."

Sudeikis then created a Ted Lasso TV series which aired on Apple TV+ from 2020-2023, winning numerous awards over its three seasons. Lasso manages AFC Richmond, who are based on the Eagles, playing in red and blue, and at 'Nelson Road', which was a digitally-transformed Selhurst Park. If you look closely, you can see the Holmesdale Road end having AFC Richmond's nickname – the Greyhounds – replace the usual 'Palace, Eagles!' seats. In the second episode of the first series, the real Crystal Palace beat AFC Richmond 4-1 'away' at Nelson Road. Lasso is asked by a journalist about the game and jokes; "A palace made out of crystal seems mighty fragile if you ask me," and as the credits roll, 'Glad All Over' is played. Former Eagles' striker Clinton Morrison also features in the series as a media pundit.

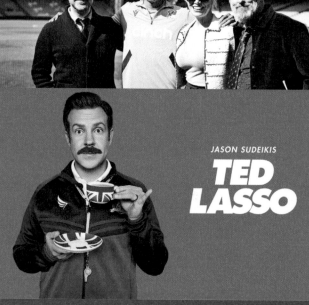

JASON SUDEIKIS

TED LASSO

Sudeikis and other actors visited Selhurst Park in April 2023 to see Palace beat West Ham 4-3, meeting Roy Hodgson and the players after the game. Fans on the official Selhurst Park tour may see some elements of Ted Lasso if they look hard enough and with AFC Richmond incorporated into the 'FIFA 23' game, you can even take charge of the Eagles and visit Selhurst Park as the away team.

CLASSIC CELEBRATIONS

TURF MOOR. 30.11.19
JEFFREY SCHLUPP
V BURNLEY

SELHURST PARK. 23.04.05
ANDY JOHNSON V LIVERPOOL

SELHURST PARK. 23.11.14
MILE JEDINAK V LIVERPOOL

SELHURST PARK. 29.03.14
JULIAN SPERONI V CHELSEA

DARREN AMBROSE
V SHEFF WEDS

HILLSBOROUGH. 02.05.10

AMEX STADIUM. 13.05.13
WILFRIED ZAHA V BRIGHTON

SELHURST PARK. 05.05.14
DWIGHT GAYLE V LIVERPOOL

SELHURST PARK. 10.04.17
JASON PUNCHEON
V NORWICH

YOHAN CABAYE
V ARSENAL

SELHURST PARK. 09.04.16

WORLD CUP PALACE

The FIFA Men's World Cup 2022 in Qatar saw Eagles defender Joachim Andersen represent Denmark and attacker Jordan Ayew play for Ghana, while Paige Bailey-Gayle pulled on the Jamaica shirt at the FIFA Women's World Cup 2023 in Australia and New Zealand.

JOACHIM ANDERSEN

Tuesday 22 November
Education City Stadium, Doha
DENMARK 0-0 TUNISIA
Played full game

Saturday 26 November
Stadium 974, Doha
FRANCE 2-1 DENMARK
Played full game

Wednesday 30 November
Al Wakrah Stadium, Doha
AUSTRALIA 1-0 DENMARK
Played full game

JORDAN AYEW

Thursday 24 November
Stadium 974, Doha
PORTUGAL 3-2 GHANA
Came on as 77th-minute substitute

Monday 28 November
Education City Stadium. Doha
SOUTH KOREA 2-3 GHANA
Subbed off in 78th-minute

Friday 2 December
Al Wakrah Stadium, Doha
GHANA 0-2 URUGUAY
Subbed off at half-time

THREE LIONS PALACE

Goalkeeper Sam Johnstone, defender Marc Guéhi and attacking midfielder Ebere Eze were all selected by England manager (and former Eagles' captain) Gareth Southgate to be part of his squad for the UEFA EURO 2024 qualifying games against Malta and North Macedonia in June 2023.

For Eze it was his senior debut while Johnstone and Guéhi added to their appearances.

It was just the third time in over 30 years that three Crystal Palace players had been selected for a senior England side.

Friday 16 June 2023
Ta' Qali National Stadium, Malta

MALTA 0-4 ENGLAND
Guéhi played full game, Eze came on as a 70th-minute substitute, Johnstone was an unused substitute.

Monday 19 June 2023
Old Trafford, Manchester
ENGLAND 7-0 NORTH MACEDONIA
All three unused substitutes.

PAIGE BAILEY-GAYLE
The Jamaican forward became the first-ever Crystal Palace FC Women's player to go to a FIFA World Cup.

Even though she did not play, she was an integral part of the Jamaica squad – the 'Reggae Girlz' – who did not concede a goal in the preliminary group and knocked out Brazil, before losing to Colombia in the last 16.

It was the first time any Jamaica team had made a FIFA World Cup knock-out round.

EZE SKILLS
BODY FEINTS

Behind Ebere Eze's skills are hours and hours of practice. Along with Dajon Golding, his childhood friend and now coach and professional footballer, Eze shows you how to get past any opposition player and help your team get up the pitch. **There are four steps to the body feint:**

1

Touch forward.

2

Step with the opposite foot to which you are going to take the ball with, lean into the direction you want the opposition player to believe you're going in.

3

Drop your shoulder, lower your centre of gravity, move body parts as well to 'sell' the action.

4

Touch to get away.

WHY DO THIS?

Dajon says: "I've watched Ebere go from dropping his shoulder and scoring worldies in our local park, to doing it in the Premier League.

"Dropping the shoulder is a key tool in your tool box if you want to get away from a defender. It's the difference between you having an extra 1-2 seconds to play that killer pass or break lines to get into the final third."

"It can be used all over the pitch from defence to attack and can be practised anytime, anywhere."

PRACTICE MAKES PERFECT

Eze says: *"Practice is very important. I've been practising since I was young. Body feints are something that have sort of grown with me and I'm so used to them. They're something I use so much; they've now become part of my game."*

"The one against Southampton when I've dropped the shoulder to go one way to get around, got a shot off and it went in. It was quite effective and that's why I like them."

EZE ON WHICH PLAYERS HE WATCHED DOING BODY FEINTS:

"Ronaldinho did a lot of skills with body feints and Lionel Messi is probably the best example of a player who does body feints but isn't really using any skills with them."

ON YOUR FEET

Dajon says: *"First, being comfortable with the ball at your feet is vital and then being able to drop the shoulder allows you the ability to get away from your defender."*

EZE ON BODY FEINTS:

"They're important because that's what I use to get past players, to destabilise them and create opportunities for myself. They're easy to do, but they're crazy effective. It's practical on the pitch. You know exactly what you want to do and the defender doesn't. It's a good way of getting past people."

EZE ON THE BEST BODY FEINTER AT PALACE:
"I'D PROBABLY SAY ME."

COACH DAJON HAS SET YOU A BODY FEINT CHALLENGE.

Start by looking in the mirror and see how you look when you drop your shoulder. Then, lower your body and plant one foot before moving an imaginary ball outside of your other foot.

When confident, introduce the ball and then test yourself in these three different scenarios:

1. Stationary ball at your feet
2. Receiving the ball: take a touch then perform shoulder drop
3. Dribbling at speed

Repeat each five times and only move onto the next one when you have completed five correctly!

ACCELERATE

Dajon says: *"Once you've feinted and beaten the defender, take your touch into space at pace then make your decision to drive, pass or shoot."*

PALACE FOR LIFE
FOUNDATION

PALACE FOR LIFE

The Palace for Life Foundation is the official charity of Crystal Palace F.C. We have been working with the south London community for over 25 years.

We use the power of football and Palace to change the lives of young people in the boroughs of Bromley, Croydon, Sutton and Lambeth and wider communities through free sporting sessions, education training and employment programmes, 1:1 mentoring and various other forms of support.

Find out more and get involved through participating in sessions, volunteering, fundraising and lots more by following us: @PalaceForLife

Made in South London: A year on...

In 2022 we launched our 'Made in South London' fundraising campaign which aimed to raise £1 million over three years to help us reach over 3,000 more young people with our existing programmes.

Actor, rapper and comedian Doc Brown helped launch the campaign by writing and starring in a video featuring Palace players in unfamiliar roles: Wilfried Zaha was a taxi driver, Joel Ward was a market seller and Marc Guéhi was a lollipop man.

Powerchair success

Our Powerchair team train in Croydon every week and won the South East Powerchair Football League second division and Fair Play Award last season. To celebrate, they were given VIP tickets for a game at Selhurst Park and even went pitchside for a picture! Palace players Vicente Guaita and Chloe Arthur have even taken part in their sessions.

Marathon March

Marathon March is a 26.2 mile charity walk around south London with all money raised going directly to us. The 2022 edition saw a record-breaking 150 people take part with nearly £85,000 raised. Why not contact us to take part in a future Marathon March? It's a fun, family-friendly event and is a chance to complete a personal challenge and raise money for a good cause.

Blind Football/Takeover Day

Every season the club hosts a Palace for Life takeover game at Selhurst Park and for the 2022/23 season fans got to try out blind football in The Fanzone, hear more about us and even had the chance to win a t-shirt from one of our t-shirt guns!

Ceren: "I want to show girls that we can play football too"

15-year-old Ceren is one of the many participants who has been positively impacted by our girls-only Kicks sessions. Ceren's dream is to become a professional footballer. She began her journey at school in South Norwood, where she developed her technical ability, enthusiasm and passion for the game. Through participating consistently at school, she was offered the opportunity to play at Palace for Life's annual Play on the Pitch event, which gave her the chance to battle it out against other schools on the pitch at Selhurst Park. Through our Kicks sessions she not only found a passion for playing but also taking on a leadership role, assisting her coaches to encourage more girls to play more football.

Tyrick Mitchell and Elise Hughes record podcast with Palace for Life participants

Palace players Tyrick and Elise joined one of our GAME ON sessions to help record a Podcast. GAME ON is an employment, training and education programme that gives young people the skills they need to take the next steps in their career. The players were asked questions like 'who is the hardest player you've ever played against?' and 'do you prefer to play club or country?', with the session filmed and broadcast on BBC oon the BBC's famous Match of the Day programme. What would you ask a player if you had a chance?

BEHIND-THE-SCENES:
PLAYER SIGNING ON SOCIAL

Crystal Palace Social Media Manager Sammy Brough reveals what happens behind-the-scenes on social when a player is signed by the club…

1. A message from our Sporting Director notifies us that we will be signing a player, information on the player is given and then the planning begins. This time it's the Brazilian, Matheus França.
2. Medical time. The player goes through various testing with our medical team to make sure all is good to go.
3. SMILE for the camera! Once our new signing is in the building it's time for some photos and a video.
4. A little bit of social content is next. Here Matheus is signing his very first Palace shirt which we will give away on social for someone to win.
5. His first words as a Palace player! Matheus speaks to Chris Grierson for Palace TV.
6. Next, he visits his new home and meets his new teammates.
7. The day is complete and we make the official announcement on all our social media channels.

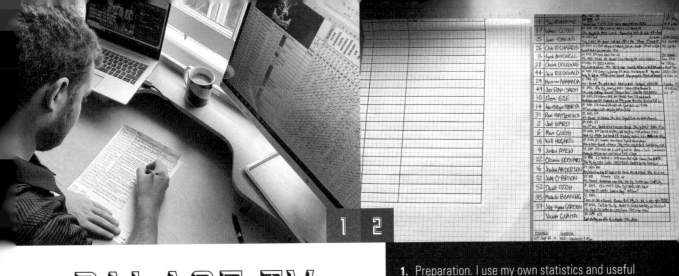

PALACE TV COMMENTARY

Club commentator Will Robinson takes us behind-the-scenes when commentating on the Eagles…

1. Preparation. I use my own statistics and useful websites to get information. Age, height, nationality, latest statistics on each player are important, plus a fun fact.
2. I write this up into these notes. When commentating, you have a split-second to locate info.
3. I get to the stadium at least two hours before kick-off and check all my equipment is working. The buttons and dials control what I hear in my headphones, like crowd noise, and they allow me talk to the director without my voice going out on air.
4. When the line-ups are announced, I highlight the starting teams in my notes and then discuss with my co-commentator what the tactics might be. Here, Palace legend Mark Bright writes the formation on a sticky note so I can attach it to my notes.
5. After my introduction to the game and team news, it's kick-off. Preparation helps, but the most important thing is describing what is happening on the pitch.
6. At full-time we summarise the game, sign off and head home. Then preparation for the next game starts again.

SPOT THE BALL

The ball has disappeared! Can you spot where it should be?

Answers on Page 61!

30

DEAN
HENDERSON

LEGO PALACE

Chris Smith is a big Lego and Crystal Palace fan. He also has a special project called 'Brickstand' which sees him build grounds and a whole lot more. He starts with getting pictures of what he is building from the internet and then, like all of us, uses trial and error to build. Chris has built a few special things for us and shows us how.

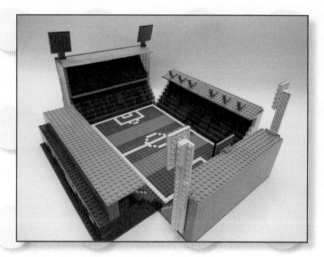

SELHURST PARK

Somewhere between 1,500-2,000 pieces were used for this, could you build it too?

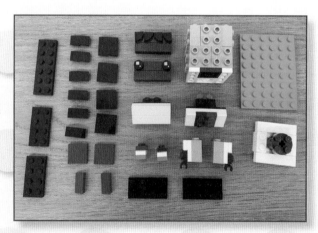

EBERE EZE

If you love Eze, Palace and Lego, then this is the perfect model to make. Can you work out how to make him using these pieces?

DUG-OUTS
This is where the managers, coaching team and substitutes sit during matches.

CHANGING ROOMS
The most secretive part of the ground on a matchday, this is where the players and managers discuss all the important things before, during and after games.

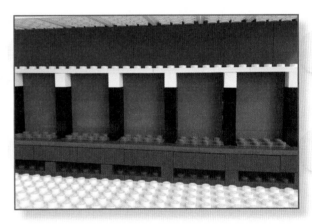

CREATE YOUR OWN PALACE HOME SHIRT DESK TIDY IN SIX EASY STEPS...
Always got pens rolling around on your desk or table and need somewhere to put them? Why not build this?

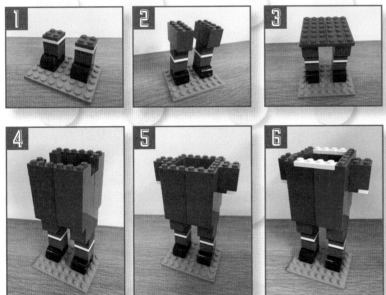

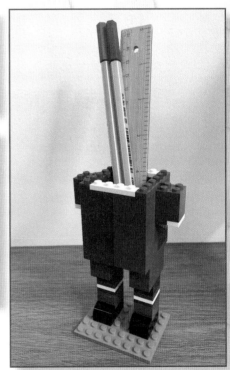

FOLLOW CHRIS AND BRICKSTAND: TWITTER @BRICKSTAND
INSTAGRAM @FCBRICKSTAND

GOODBYE AND THANKS!

At the end of the 2022/23 season, we said goodbye to some important names involved with the club in recent years. Thanks to all of them for their hard work and ensuring the club had special memories along the way.

WILFRIED ZAHA

Position: Attacker
First game for Palace: vs Cardiff City (h) 1-2 27/03/10
Last game for Palace: vs Bournemouth (h) 2-0 13/05/23
Appearances: 458
Goals: 90
International: Cote d'Ivoire

at Manchester United and Cardiff City from 29/05/13-27/08/14

DID YOU KNOW?

Wilf lived very close to the ground after moving to England from Cote d'Ivoire as a kid. He joined Palace as an eight-year-old and was captain in his last-ever game for the club. To commemorate his service to the Eagles, the club had a mural painted on the wall of a house right next to Selhurst Park.

DANNY YOUNG

...and a special mention must also go to Danny Young.

Young joined Palace in November 2013 as Head of Kit and absorbed the role of Player Liaison four years later. He then took on the role of 'Head of Player Care', where he looked after all the professional players off the pitch so they could focus while on it.

In 2022 he received the Chairman's Award for Outstanding Contribution at the End of Season Awards.

LUKA MILIVOJEVIĆ

Position: Midfielder
Signed: 31/01/17
First game for Palace: vs Stoke City (a) 0-1 11/02/17
Last game for Palace: vs West Ham United (h) 4-3 29/04/23
Appearances: 198
Goals: 29
International: Serbia

DID YOU KNOW?

Luka was signed by Sam Allardyce on the January 2017 deadline day and quickly became club captain.

JAMES MCARTHUR

Position: Midfielder
Signed: 01/09/14
First game for Palace: vs Burnley (h) 0-0 13/09/14
Last game for Palace: vs Nottingham Forest (h) 1-1 28/05/23
Appearances: 253
Goals: 19
International: Scotland

DID YOU KNOW?

'Macca' was a long-time captain of the club and won the FA Cup with Wigan before joining Palace.

JACK BUTLAND

Position: Goalkeeper
Signed: 16/10/20
First game for Palace: vs Wolverhampton Wanderers (a) 0-1 08/01/21
Last game for Palace: vs Everton (a) 2-3 19/05/22
Appearances: 17
International: England

DID YOU KNOW?

Despite playing less than 20 times for the club, Butland helped the Eagles get to just their fifth-ever FA Cup semi-final as a professional club, when he played in all five games in their 2021/22 cup run which saw them lose against Chelsea at Wembley in the last four.

THE ART OF THE ASSIST
MICHAEL OLISE

The 2022/23 Premier League season saw Michael Olise make 11 assists in his 37 Premier League games for the Eagles. When he delivered an inch-perfect cross-field pass to Ebere Eze to score against Bournemouth on 13 May 2023 at Selhurst Park, Olise wrote himself into the Palace history books.

He became the first Eagle to reach double figures for assists in the Premier League and two weeks later he got his 11th and final one of a successful season.

Olise's 11 assists saw him overtake Wilfried Zaha (2016/17) and Wayne Routledge (2004/05) who both made nine assists in a season.

Using his left foot every time, here are all of Michael Olise's 2022/23 assists… which one was your favourite?

9. to Jordan Ayew vs West Ham (h) 29/04/23 (4-3).

1. to Odsonne Edouard vs Leeds (h) 09/10/22 (2-1)

2. to Ebere Eze vs Wolverhampton Wanderers (h) 18/10/22 (2-1)

3. to Jordan Ayew vs Bournemouth (a) 31/12/22 (2-0)

4. to Ebere Eze vs Bournemouth (a) 31/12/22 (2-0)

5. to Ebere Eze vs Brentford (a) 18/02/23 (1-1)

6. to Jordan Ayew vs Leeds (a) 09/04/23 (5-1)

7. to Ebere Eze vs Leeds (a) 09/04/23 (5-1)

8. to Odsonne Edouard vs Leeds (a) 09/04/23 (5-1)

10. to Ebere Eze vs Bournemouth (h) 13/05/23 (2-0)

11. to Will Hughes vs Nottingham Forest (h) 28/05/23 (1-1)

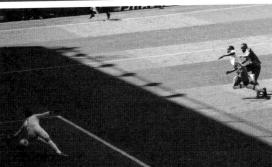

SINCE THE PROFESSIONAL CLUB OF CRYSTAL PALACE F.C. WAS FORMED IN 1905 THERE HAVE BEEN OVER 50 DIFFERENT NAMES IN THE MANAGERIAL HOT SEAT.

WE TAKE A LOOK AT SOME KEY NAMES OVER THAT HISTORY.

JOHN ROBSON (1905-07)

- first-ever manager of the present-day Eagles
- won Southern League Second Division in first season
- provided one of the first-ever club shocks – defeating Newcastle to reach FA Cup quarter-finals

EDMUND GOODMAN (1907-1925)

- helped set up club in 1905 after moving from Aston Villa
- took over from Robson as manager in 1907
- longest-serving manager in history of club with over 600 competitive games
- was at club in various roles before retiring in 1933, a total of 28 years

BERT HEAD (1966-73)

- got club promoted to the top-flight – First Division (now Premier League) – for the first time

MALCOLM ALLISON (1973-76, 1980-81)

- joined in March 1973, changed club nickname to 'Eagles' from 'Glaziers' and club shirts to red and blue stripes
- led club to their first-ever FA Cup semi-final in the 1975/76 season

TERRY VENABLES (1976-80, 1998-99)

- former Palace player got team promoted to Second Division in 1976/77
- won promotion to the top-flight at Selhurst Park with win against Burnley in May 1979 witnessed by a record 51,482 fans
- only Palace manager to manage team in a UEFA competition, when the Eagles played Samsunspor in the UEFA Intertoto Cup

STEVE KEMBER (1981-82, 2001, 2003)

- former player and youth team coach took over in November 1981 and kept team up in Second Division
- returned as manager in April 2001 and kept the club in the First Division
- returned as manager in 2003, leading club to top of First Division

STEVE COPPELL (1984-93, 1995-96, 1997-98, 1999-00)

- became youngest manager in Football League after joining in June 1984
- longest-serving Palace manager post-Second World War
- led team to FA Cup Final, top-three finish in top-flight and Full Members Cup title at Wembley

PALACE HISTORY: THE MANAGERS

ALAN SMITH (1993-95, 2000-01)
- joined Eagles in November 1983 as youth team manager, later becoming reserve team manager and assistant manager
- won the 1993/94 First Division title with team captained by Gareth Southgate
- took Eagles to both the League and FA Cup semi-finals in 1994/95

ATTILIO LOMBARDO (1998)
- Italian became first non-British manager of the club in March 1998
- Youngest-ever Premier League manager at the time (32)
- As player-manager, was assisted by fellow player Tomas Brolin with translation duties

IAIN DOWIE (2003-06)
- former player who joined from Oldham in December 2003
- guided team one place off the bottom of the First Division to 14 victories in their next 23 games to make play-offs
- won promotion to Premier League after defeating West Ham in play-off final

PAUL HART (2010)
- joined club in administration and appointed Dougie Freedman as assistant
- ensured club were not relegated to the third tier (League One) for the first time since 1976/77

ALAN PARDEW (2015-16)
- former player, joined as manager in January 2015 and led club to a top-10 finish, the highest-ever Premier League finish
- guided club to FA Cup Final against Manchester United at Wembley in May 2016

PATRICK VIEIRA (2021-23)
- first-ever FIFA World Cup winner to manage the Eagles
- the Frenchman guided club to fifth FA Cup semi-final and 12th-place Premier League finish in first season

ROY HODGSON (2017-21, 2023-)
- born in Croydon and former schoolboy player of the Eagles
- joined Palace in September 2017 as manager and led them to an 11th place finish
- in his second season equalled best-ever points total in a single Premier League campaign (49)
- left club in May 2021, before returning in April 2023 to guide them away from relegation

COLOUR IN

Pete and Alice the Eagle are the Official Crystal Palace F.C. Mascots who have been keeping fans of all ages entertained at Selhurst Park for many years.

Pete wears Number 18 on his back and Alice Number 61. Together they are '1861' – the year the amateur club was founded.

Give them some colour and why not colour in the club logo too…

SPOT THE DIFFERENCE

Can you spot the eight differences between these two photos?

Answers on Page 61!

THE FANS

Together, we are South London and Proud.

B

C

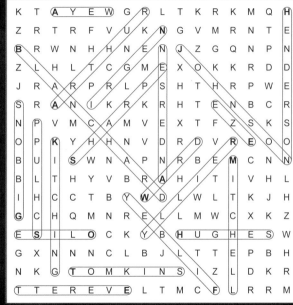

CAN YOU FIND PETE AND ALICE THE EAGLE?